Nurse Tools

by Laura Hamilton Waxman

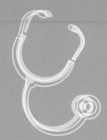

BUMBA BOOKS™

LERNER PUBLICATIONS ◆ MINNEAPOLIS

Note to Educators

Throughout this book, you'll find critical-thinking questions. These can be used to engage young readers in thinking critically about the topic and in using the text and photos to do so.

Lerner Publications Company
A division of Lerner Publishing Group, Inc.
241 First Avenue North
Minneapolis, MN 55401 USA

For reading levels and more information, look up this title at www.lernerbooks.com.

Main body text set in Helvetica Textbook Com Roman 23/49.
Typeface provided by Linotype AG.

Library of Congress Cataloging-in-Publication Data

Names: Waxman, Laura Hamilton, author.
Title: Nurse tools / Laura Hamilton Waxman.
Description: Minneapolis : Lerner Publications, [2020] | Series: Bumba Books—Community helpers tools of the trade | Audience: Age 4–7. | Audience: K to Grade 3. | Includes bibliographical references and index.
Identifiers: LCCN 2018043225 (print) | LCCN 2018043974 (ebook) | ISBN 9781541557352 (eb pdf) | ISBN 9781541557321 (lb : alk. paper)
Subjects: LCSH: Nurses—Juvenile literature. | Nursing—Juvenile literature.
Classification: LCC RT61.5 (ebook) | LCC RT61.5 .W39 2020 (print) | DDC 610.73—dc23

LC record available at https://lccn.loc.gov/2018043225

Manufactured in the United States of America
1-46147-45896-11/8/2018

Table of
Contents

Let's Visit a Nurse!

Nurses help keep people healthy.

They use many tools to do their job.

Nurses see patients in hospitals and doctors' offices.

They wear clothes called scrubs.

Sometimes they wear gloves.

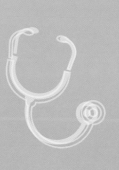

Where else do nurses work?

Nurses use a scale.

It measures your weight.

A ruler measures your height.

Why do you think nurses check your weight and height?

A small light helps nurses

look at your eyes.

Nurses also use the light to

check inside your mouth.

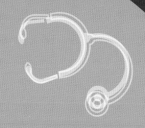

Nurses check how well

a patient hears.

They use a special tool

for this job.

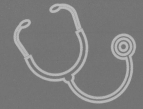

Nurses use another tool to

listen to your heartbeat.

They also listen to your lungs.

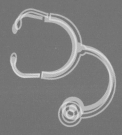

15

A nurse might give you a shot.

Shots help keep you healthy.

Nurses use bandages for someone who is cut or hurt. The bandages help to keep out germs.

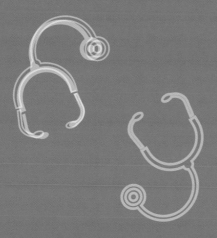

Nurses use many tools

to help their patients.

They help us all stay well!

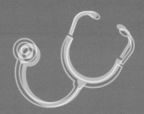

Nurse Tools

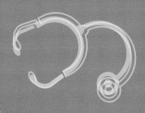

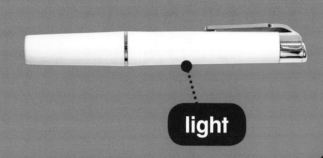

light

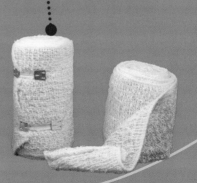

scrubs

scale

bandages

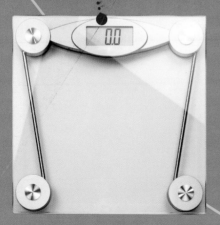

Picture Glossary

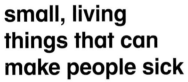

germs

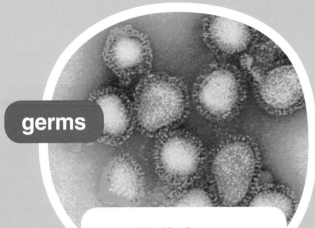

small, living things that can make people sick

lungs

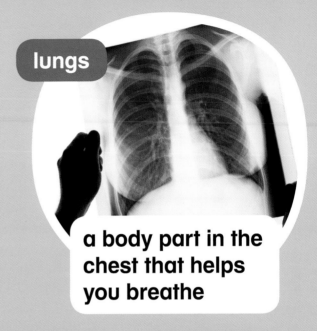

a body part in the chest that helps you breathe

measures

finds out the size or weight of someone

patients

people who visit a nurse

23

Read More

Arnold, Quinn M. *Nurses.* Mankato, MN: Creative Education, 2017.

Meister, Cari. *Nurses.* Minneapolis: Bullfrog Books, 2015.

Parkes, Elle. *Hooray for Nurses!* Minneapolis: Lerner Publications, 2017.

Index

Photo Credits

Image credits: Minerva Studio/Shutterstock.com, p. 5; Monkey Business Images/Shutterstock.com, pp. 6–7, 23; Steve Hix/Fuse/Getty Images, p. 8; Terry Vine/Getty Images, pp. 10–11, 23; singkamc/Getty Images, p. 12; ziviani/Shutterstock.com, p. 15; FatCamera/Getty Images, p. 16; SelectStock/Getty Images, p. 18; Pressmaster/Shutterstock.com, p. 20; Garrett Aitken/Shutterstock.com, p. 22; Steve Heap/Shutterstock.com, p. 22; AnggunFaith/Shutterstock.com, p. 22; oonal/Getty Images, p. 22; Caspar Benson/Getty Images, p. 23; CDC/SCIENCE PHOTO LIBRARY/Getty Images, p. 23; Steve Hix/Fuse/Getty Images, p. 23.

Cover Images: De Space Studio/Shutterstock.com; VGstockstudio/Shutterstock.com; Canoneer/Shutterstock.com.